Victoria

Intimate Home

~ Creating a Private World ~

Victoria

Intimate Home

~ Creating a Private World ~

HEARST BOOKS

New York

Copyright notices, permissions, and acknowledgments appear
on pages 110-111.

Library of Congress Catalog Card Number: 91-16562
ISBN: 0-688-09739-1

Printed in Singapore
First Edition
2 3 4 5 6 7 8 9 10

www.williammorrow.com

For Victoria:
Nancy Lindemeyer, Editor
Susan Maher, Art Director
John Mack Carter, President, Hearst Magazine Enterprises

Produced by Smallwood & Stewart, Inc., New York City

Edited by Alice Wong
Designed by Barbara Scott-Goodman
Text by Catherine Revland with Linda Sunshine

NOTICE: Every effort has been made to locate the copyright
owners of the material used in this book. Please let us know if
an error has been made, and we will make any necessary
changes in subsequent printings.

CONTENTS

FOREWORD

One of the blessings of my growing-up years was having places in our home that were just mine. Or at least that is how I felt about them. Of course I had a room, but when I was very little that was shared with my older sister. It was not my bedroom, however, that became a place in my heart, it was the windy little stairway that led to my room.

Our home was a Queen Anne Victorian which seemed to me to have spaces and rooms that were enormous. We had a parlor and a living room, and right off the dining room was a divine little sewing room. At the back of the kitchen was my magical stairway. On the bottom steps my grandmother often stored such things as tins of cookies and crocks where fruitcakes were basted with brandy waiting for the holidays. After school, I perched here, often until dinner time reading library books or just dreaming. At the top of the stairs was a landing, another secret spot, and beyond that the attic where I was the sole occupant for such enterprises as my editorial office or some other girlhood scenario.

I have never forgotten those precious hours in these secret, just-mine places where imagination had room to grow. This is the spirit I try to maintain in my home, and the places where I find special solace and peace, while not nearly as enchanting, are still the favorite parts of the house.

The very heart of home is intimacy. For this is where we are the most ourselves. And when we have that inner calm, that is when we give the best parts of ourselves. A chair in a sunny corner where a child can learn to read, and later, perhaps, tell a secret or discuss a problem—that is the essence of what this volume is all about. We hope that you will enjoy the quiet times of this book—it is one of sharing the true meaning and wonder of home.

Nancy Lindemeyer, Editor, *Victoria*

INTRODUCTION

In the midst of today's hectic living, there still can exist in our homes a haven where we can savor the simple and charming things in life. In the pages of *Intimate Home*, the editors of *Victoria* celebrate the everyday eloquence of life's small domestic rituals. From bathing and dressing in the morning to falling into slumber in the evening, these intimate spaces evoke a graceful world, one with time set aside for leisure and gentility.

In the past, much of life was centered in the home with its many tempting private spaces. The unique architecture of Victorian houses provided for nooks under steeply sloping rafters and gables, or hideaways at the tops of the stairs. In this same spirit, dozens of lovely refuges that can be created in today's houses and apartments are offered in *Intimate Home*. Here one can seek momentary sanctuary from the rigors of the day, relax and read or merely let the mind wander. Here one may be inspired to write or to paint, or perhaps to excel at the domestic arts. Here one can retire at the end of the day, to sleep the deep sleep of childhood and rise to greet the soft light of day through a veil of lace. Here one will bathe and dress in comfort and unhurried pleasure.

A small space is not necessarily an intimate one, but it can be made so by the presence of favorite things. Some objects are valued heirlooms, and others the rewards of a lifetime of wandering through little back street shops and yard sales, searching out those neglected treasures that call to us in quiet voices. Such blessings are candidly displayed to be admired each day.

Of the brief but happy years of Queen Victoria's marriage to her beloved Albert, the poet and Queen's biographer, Dame Edith Sitwell, remarked: "Life has become a round of simple pleasures and domestic delights." *Intimate Home* is a celebration of those mundane pleasures, in photographs, text, and excerpts from the writings of Saki, Henry James, Jane Austen, Daphne du Maurier, and of course, Virginia Woolf, who first championed the idea that women had a sacred right to what they yearned for—the frequent pleasure of their own company. Together they pay homage to a belief in the beauty of all things, and to a joyful love of life with its daily "round of simple pleasures and domestic delights."

A PLACE FOR SOLITUDE

*t*he nineteenth-century poet William Wordsworth wrote, "When from our better selves we have too long been parted . . . how gracious, how benign, is Solitude." And how thoroughly pleasing it is to meet up with one's better self in a small sanctuary designed for a peaceful respite, for meditation, or as a reader's roost where, transported through books to faraway places, one can take frequent journeys of the spirit.

Within these pages are many oases of serenity in which to enjoy the grace of solitude. The old-fashioned home, of course, is particularly suited to this pursuit. Its delightful irregularity produces rooms full of odd angles and gentle curves. Under the eaves where breezes brush the treetops, in hidden bays and recesses, or in rooms with steeply sloped walls are natural sanctuaries. In these nooks and corners a woman can create a place to call her own, in the company of her thoughts and dreams. To reflect and gather strength from deep within or to imagine and soar with the mind, a private space is essential to the soul. And from it, one emerges revitalized with a new sense of peace, ready to embrace the world once again.

This chapter is devoted to the room that invites the companionableness of solitude, a gentle room washed with light or lace-dappled shade where nothing overwhelms and all elements blend harmoniously. It is a place where linen with its ethereal sheen heightens the rich ruby of a Turkish carpet, or it is a pristine whitewashed loft of a nineteenth-century barn, a painter's canvas drop cloth thrown over a sofa. Or it is simplicity itself: a white couch, a spray of dogwood, and honeyed light. In rooms such as these Virginia Woolf could happily pursue her own need for quietude, in which she could "dream over books . . . and let the line of thought dip deeper into the stream." One may call that solitude; another calls it peace.

E nchanting words and magical stories by great writers are at home in this little nook, left, ensconced in a corner of a room.

Embroidered linens and vintage laces add a serene quality. The filet crochet piece atop the bed reveals a winter woodland scene.

It was broad daylight when Anne awoke and
sat up in bed, staring confusedly at the window
through which a flood of cheery sunshine was
pouring and outside of which something white
and feathery waved across glimpses of blue
sky. . . . This was Green Gables . . . it was
morning and, yes, it was a cherry-tree in full
bloom outside of her window. . . . Oh, wasn't it
beautiful? Wasn't it a lovely place? Suppose she
wasn't really going to stay here! She would
imagine she was. There was scope for imagination here. . . .

On both sides of the house was a big orchard,
one of apple trees and one of cherry trees, also
showered over with blossoms; and their grass was
all sprinkled with dandelions. In the garden be-
low were lilac trees purple with flowers, and
their dizzily sweet fragrance drifted up to the
window on the morning wind. . . .

Anne's beauty-loving eyes lingered on it all,
taking everything greedily in; she had looked on
so many unlovely places in her life, poor child;
but this was as lovely as anything she had ever
dreamed.

L. M. Montgomery
Anne of Green Gables

R oses all but climb the rustic whitewashed
rafters of this country attic, a whimsical
doll-like house in palest pink and white that
transports the occupant back to a rural childhood. Informality reigns, the garage-sale chic
offset by the elegance of the vintage florals and
prized collection of red and white willoware.

Crisscross curtains that billow deeply adorn slate blue French windows, above, and soften the sunlight in this beguiling reading area. ❧ In a gabled room at the top of a house, right, fond remembrances can be artfully re-created. Flowers are everywhere, painting a vision as lovely as a garden, and creating a bedroom for dreams to bloom in as beautifully.

A VIEW OF NATURE

Sweet serenity is the overall impression of a house nestled into a hill overlooking San Francisco Bay. Built in 1896, this Victorian has been cared for by six families. The present owner is a printmaker who appreciates its tranquil setting and exquisite vista. "It's always been a place that's loved by the people who live here," she explains. "The house itself is wonderful, but the location is also so special. Life is ever-changing when you live by the water."

It is by the water that the owner resides with her husband, son, and two Airedale pups. To the combination of Victorian charm in the midst of Californian hillside and waters, the owner has added her personal touch. All around the house are objects she has inherited or created. As a printmaker, she produces delicate pieces that express her love of pattern and color, as well as give testimony to her heritage. Receiving inspiration from quilting patterns, the artist prints similar creations onto paper, replicating the texture of the fabrics by also embossing the work. Her prints hang side by side with needleworks made by the women in her ancestry. "I'm part of a long line of quilters from the past. Seeing what has been done before can inspire me."

With the many hours spent on her work, this artist also desires a place for rest. Though it is in the den that she quilts with her family around her, and beneath the eaves in the attic studio that she works, there are other favorite spots. The house offers numerous breathtaking views of the water and of the surrounding garden from its front porch and from its many windows. In these areas the artist takes refreshing breaks from her work. No matter what the weather, the view from the house never fails to soothe. "Nature always speaks to me but never requires an answer. It always fills my mind with peace and joy," she says.

One particular refuge that this artist has grown to love is in the corner of the master bedroom. Here, a window seat follows the gentle curve of the irregular windows. The lofty ceiling allows for windows with an expansive view of her garden and of the bay beyond it. "Over the years this has become my special retreat. The printmaking I do requires intense concentration and a lot of eyestrain. I take several breaks a day just to sit and stare," she explains. "I don't know why, but watching the graceful way trees sway in the breeze provides me with an immediate calming effect. And no matter how often I look out on the garden and water, there is something new happening. Nature never stops changing, and I have learned to value that adaptability in my own life."

From the window seat that follows the gentle flow of the bay, right, nature's daily changes can be observed. The tranquility of wild and domesticated growing things in the fullness of their natural beauty pervades this place for solitude.

An all-white room has a serenely calming effect. In the absence of color, texture and shape are all—as in the ruching on the graceful loveseat and the alluring jacquard weave of the lady's wing chair, left. The carpet is dramatically textured with a petitpoint-and-honeycomb pattern. The pillow on the slender chair, above, is embroidered drawn-work. The delicately chain stitched linen table-cloth is strewn with lacy flowers. In this sooth-ing setting, barely touched by color, the eye and then the mind are quieted and refreshed.

W̶hat I mean by reading is not skimming, not
being able to say as the world saith, "Oh, yes, I've read that!,"
but reading again and again, in all sorts of moods,
with an increase of delight every time, till the thing read has become
a part of your system and goes forth along with you to meet
any new experience you may have.

C. E. Montague
A Writer's Notes on His Trade

Meditative places need a personal imprint such as the intriguing mixture of opulence and whimsy, left, with lush damask walls, elegant appointments, and unusually bright colors of bittersweet red and yellow. The amusing painted dog and green silk candlestick lamp shade trimmed in black velvet complete a scene to inspire the solitary imagination.

Henry David Thoreau once asked in his essay "Reading": "How many a man has dated a new era in his life from the reading of a book?" A quiet and soothing corner for undisturbed reading is one of the great necessities of life. Favorite volumes should be kept in plain sight, where one can turn to them often for guidance and inspiration. Charming Grecian busts, above, are used as bookends for treasured volumes of poetry.

THE EARLY MORNING HOURS

Time alone for the owner of a flower shop in a small fishing village means waking before sunrise to spend the first few precious hours of the day in quiet contemplation. "Everyone asks me why, and the answer is so simple," she explains. "It's a joy to wake up in the morning just before the sun. Then I get back into bed with a hot cup of coffee and just breathe. Those first few hours are so pristine and fresh, I find them the best part of the day. The more time I can get in then, the better my day is."

One of the joys of her early morning solitude is the quality of Rhode Island light reflecting off the ocean and the bay, which streams in the numerous windows of the house. As her bed-room faces north, she is able to observe both sunrise and sunset, and loves to watch the way the varying rays fill her whitewashed home with subtle color.

The serenity she enjoys each morning is also enhanced by the spare simplicity of her nearly two-hundred-year-old house. "I put in twelve-hour days at my flower shop, where life is hectic nearly all year. In my bedroom I don't have a television or a telephone or even a closet, just a bed and an Ad-irondack chair. To me the bed-room is for rest, and for watch-ing the endless changes of nature going on outside my window," she states. "At home I need a very peaceful environment."

She creates this environment by decorating with live topi-aries and dried flower sculp-tures. The brick wall she un-covered behind an old fireplace became a splendid backdrop for lots of greenery. Her many windows are sites for window boxes and a collection of "mossy old flower pots" planted with miniature roses and other favorites. Simple wooden chairs are always placed in these sun-splashed areas. Here, the chairs welcome one to enjoy a view of her blooming garden, or serve as display pedestals for a tub of lavender and other arrangements. A table by another win-dow is a favorite spot for early morning paper-work or a breakfast with the sun. With so many parts of the house graced with simply a piece of furniture, a pot of flowers, and a view, it is evident that its occupant is a person with a love of nature and of peace.

The energy of the sun nurtures the mind and soul as well as plants. In the bright area at the top of the stairs, above, is a table for work or breakfast. ❧ The brick wall and foliage, right, create a rustic spot for tranquil moments perfumed with roses.

*L*et us have a quiet hour. . . .

Alfred, Lord Tennyson

The delicate creamy yellow of the dogwood is reflected in the linens and light quality of this inviting corner with its pleasing textures of crisply pleated borders and richly embossed embroideries. Here is a place where one could be mindful of Virginia Woolf's advice for achieving a tranquil mind: to "pluck the petals from a rose or watch a swan float calmly down a river."

A place for contemplation is a back porch, left, with quaint gingerbread railing, traditional "porch gray" painted floor, and, of course, wicker. Here pleasant afternoons are spent sipping a cup of tea and watching butterflies play. Gentle evenings under the flicker of a hurricane lamp and with crickets on chorus are as bewitching. ❧ A book that lies invitingly open, sprigs of Queen Anne's lace picked during a forenoon walk through a meadow, and a fresh breeze billowing the sheers, above, recall an afternoon's hour of quietude.

*F*or now she need not think about anybody. She could be herself, by herself. And that was what now she often felt the need of—to think; well, not even to think. To be silent; to be alone. All the being and the doing, expansive, glittering, vocal, evaporated; and one shrunk, with a sense of solemnity, to being oneself, a wedge-shaped core of darkness, something invisible to others. Although she continued to knit, and sat upright, it was thus that she felt herself; and this self having shed its attachments was free for the strangest adventures. When life sank down for a moment, the range of experience seemed limitless. . . . Her horizon seemed to her limitless. There were all the places she had not seen; the Indian plains; she felt herself pushing aside the thick leather curtain of a church in Rome. This core of darkness could go anywhere, for no one saw it. They could not stop it, she thought, exulting. There was freedom, there was peace, there was, most welcome of all, a summoning together, a resting on a platform of stability. Not as

oneself did one find rest ever, in her experience (she accomplished here something dexterous with her needles) but as a wedge of darkness. Losing personality, one lost the fret, the hurry, the stir; and there rose to her lips always some exclamation of triumph over life when things came together in this peace, this rest, this eternity.

Virginia Woolf
To the Lighthouse

---

*I*n "The Habit of Perfection," the nineteenth-century English poet Gerard Manley Hopkins writes: "Elected silence, sing to me . . . The music that I care to hear." Silence and solitude are a natural pair, and to all those who seek precious moments alone, silence can be as well-loved as music from a melodeon, above, still found in Louisa May Alcott's home. Over the instrument hangs a picture of the writer's sister Elizabeth, on whom she modeled the quiet and peace-loving Beth March of *Little Women*.

🐦 In an intimate corner, right, a present-day artist expresses her love of color and texture through the furnishings she has chosen. A photographer whose mother and grandmother are painters, she prefers a camera to a brush. But no matter the form an artist chooses to express a talent, she can always appreciate the restorative nature of solitude. Even with her prodigious energy, writer Jane Austen could still advocate: "To sit in idleness over a good fire in a well-proportioned room is a luxurious sensation."

A PLACE FOR PERSONAL PURSUITS

*l*ucky is the woman who courts the muse at home, for in the process she provides a daily atmosphere for herself that is both stimulating and serene, one in which her creative talents can grow and flourish. Such a place, described by Louisa May Alcott as "a little kingdom I possess, where thoughts and feelings dwell," answers the deep hunger of all those with artistic pursuits.

In the past, rare was the woman who expressed her creativity outside the home. As Virginia Woolf commented: "One has only to go into any room in any street for the whole of that extremely complex force of femininity to fly in one's face. How should it be otherwise? For women have sat indoors all these millions of years, so that by this time, the very walls are permeated by their creative force." Gifted women poured their talents into the domestic arts, becoming superlative cooks, seamstresses, letter writers, and flower growers.

Equally as rare was the woman who had a room of her own. Jane Austen wrote on a small desk drawn as close to the hearth as the fire would permit. Rosa Bonheur painted by the stove, and Mary Cassatt in a swirl of activity she described as one of "housekeeping, painting and oyster frying." Charlotte Brontë plotted her stories while mending stockings in the parsonage, and her sister Emily read while baking.

Obviously a room of one's own is not essential to the creative act, but one can imagine how these women would yearn for the private spaces shown within these pages, inviting enough to attract even the most reluctant muse, and well provided with storage for necessary tools: drawers for papers, baskets for yarn, or shelves for seedling pots and mixing bowls. In all its many forms, creating at home is performed with reverence for the beauty of the mundane, elevating everyday tasks into a gentle art.

A warm and welcoming Swedish desk beside a bed is well suited to answering correspondence and keeping diaries in privacy.

The writing surface tips up to conceal itself when not in use. Photographs, fruits, and flowers complete the charming setting.

*T*his was a woman's room, graceful, fragile,
the room of someone who had chosen every parti-
cle of furniture with great care, so that each chair,
each vase, each small, infinitesimal thing should
be in harmony with one another, and with her
own personality. It was as though she who had
arranged this room had said: "This I will have,
and this, and this," taking piece by piece from
the treasures in Manderley each object that
pleased her best, ignoring the second-rate, the
mediocre, laying her hand with sure and certain
instinct only upon the best. . . . I went and sat
down at the writing desk, and I thought how
strange it was that this room, so lovely and so
rich in colour, should be at the same time, so
business-like and purposeful. . . . But this
writing-table, beautiful as it was, was no pretty
toy where a woman would scribble little notes,
nibbling the end of a pen, leaving it, day after
day, in carelessness, the blotter a little askew.
The pigeon-holes were docketed, "letters-
unanswered," "letters-to-keep," "household,"
"estate," "menus," "miscellaneous," "addresses";
each ticket written in that same scrawling pointed
hand that I knew already.

Daphne du Maurier
Rebecca

A place for everything and everything in its
place is one of the most conducive ways
to inspire creativity. The many drawers, cubby
holes, and recesses of a Queen Anne lady's
writing desk, right, allow for accessibility. Such
venerable writing pieces often have nearly un-
detectable hideaways for special keepsakes.

*W*hat cannot letters inspire? They have souls; they can speak;
they have in them all that force which expresses the transports of the heart;
they have all the fire of our passions.
They can raise them as much as if the persons themselves were present. . . .
Having lost the substantial pleasures of seeing and possessing you,
I shall in some measure compensate this loss by the satisfaction I shall find in your writing.
There I shall read your most sacred thoughts.

From a letter of Héloïse to Abélard

A retreat, left, can be created simply by a well-placed screen, a versatile aid for stretching room space. Lofty thoughts could not help but be encouraged under an arched ceiling where the mind is quieted and allowed to occupy itself fully with the challenging task of arranging words on paper. ❧ The demilune writing table, above, looks as if it is a contemporary of the old-fashioned typewriter, but it is new, a product of the owner's line of traditional furniture. The wall covering of nostalgic sweet peas and forget-me-nots was also designed by the owner, inspired by visions of her mother's New England flower garden. The painting was picked up at a Paris flea market. All together, this alluring tableau provides her with a surrounding both familiar and stimulating when she sits down for an hour's work.

THE SOURCE OF INSPIRATION

In a New York City loft, a designer of needlework and fabric fills every corner with objects that nourish her soul and inspire her work. In her home, where she works, there are piles of books, tables and cabinets of trinkets and collectibles, baskets of fabric remnants, and a scrap wall of prints and illustrations. She describes how her gathering of disparate things is the source of her creative inspirations, "the hodgepodge that talks to me." She can never anticipate when her glance will stray to an item that will spark a project or design, and admits that her possessions are the stuff of imagination.

A piece of filet crochet her mother had saved served as a building block for one of the artist's more recent works. She adapted the old-fashioned motif of the crochet and translated it into needlepoint, creating a beautiful flower basket design. Needlepoint has been a passion of hers since she was very young. "I tried making filet lace once and left before the lesson was over because the work nearly drove me wild. It was too itsy-bitsy for my temperament," she explains. "But with needlework I'll go to the smallest point there is and won't mind at all. In fact, I love it." The needlework she loves is displayed on pillows, chair cushions, and footstool covers all over her loft.

As an artist who has freelanced at home for many years, she finds that her work habits must be unstructured. Some days she will work around the clock, inspired by the pattern of a piece of old fabric or a book cover, then take the next day to restore herself and wait for another inspiration. The baskets of yarn and needlepoint in progress scattered near favorite chairs are evidence that this artist's busy hands are never still for long. Surrounded by beautiful things that speak to her in a unique language she understands, this creative person is rarely without ideas for a new project, and considers herself blessed to be making a business out of a lifelong passion.

The pair of needlepoint pillows, above, was created by an artist who fills her home with objects that inspire her work.

🌺 A variation of the basket motif appears on the footstool, right. "I can never do a design exactly the same way twice," the artist explains.

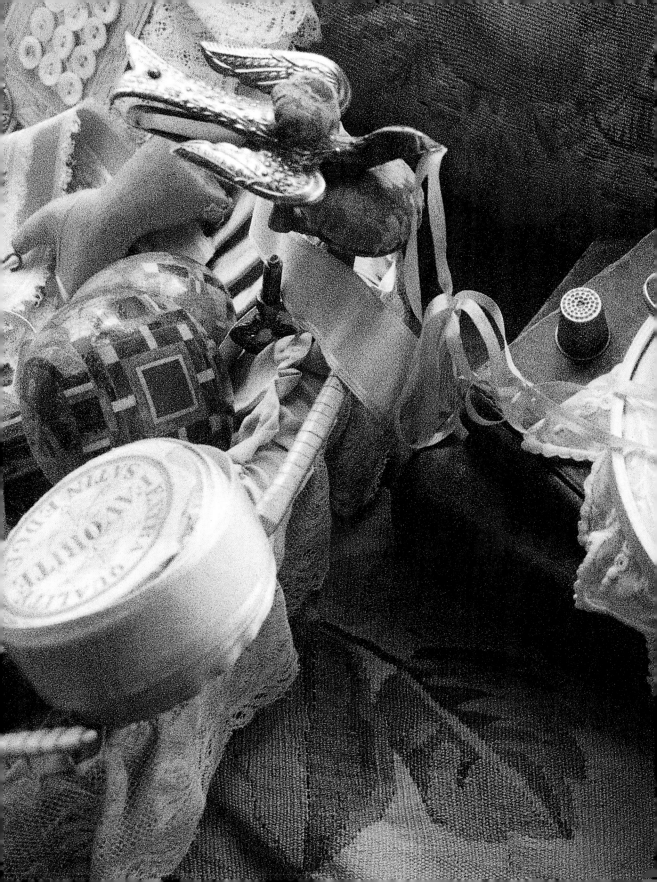

*I*t is a token of healthy and gentle characteristics,
when women of high thoughts and accomplishments
love to sew; especially as they are never more at
home with their own hearts than while so occupied.

Nathaniel Hawthorne
The Marble Faun

An embroidery hoop is like a painter's
canvas stretcher, across which the bas-
relief of a needle artist is revealed. How reward-
ing it is to spend an hour with the slenderest
needle and silken thread repairing the dainty
buds and blossoms of a treasured piece of vintage embroidery. In the catching up of old un-
ravelings, the mind follows suit and becomes
serenely untangled. Nearby, a lace-lined sewing
box is filled with charming notions and sewing
accoutrements, rolls of luscious satin edging,
and inlaid darner's rounds for the long-lost art of
mending. A hovering bird pincushion holds a
bit of ribbon in its mouth, awaiting the employ-
ment of the skillful seamstress' hand.

The art of needlecraft is one that never fails to offer immediate satisfaction, both in the doing and in the finished product, and recalls for many a woman the creative artistry of her ancestors, who poured their desires for beauty into needle, thread, and cloth. In a basement laundry, left, the air redolent of soap and streaming with sunlight, a husband and wife restore precious old linens rescued from flea markets and yard sales. The sewing machine was bought in 1945 by the wife's mother, who then taught all four of her daughters how to sew. It still performs beautifully. "I have another new and sophisticated machine that does all sorts of clever tricks," says the wife, "but it doesn't sew like this wonderful old workhorse." A tablecloth of cutwork linen and crochet found at a junk store is to be repaired. ❧ The accomplished seamstress can rescue beauty from the most unlikely places, and keeps a practiced eye out for antique buttons, frogs, ribbons, rounds of brocade trim, thimbles, seam gauges, embroidery scissors, measuring tapes, and other vintage notions, above left, for her sewing basket. She is thus ready to restore a piece of handiwork to its former glory, or add a bit of sentiment to something new. ❧ Sweet satin strawberries and a highly stylized antique lady's high top shoe, above right, are fascinating versions of the ubiquitous tomato pincushion, and a magnificent black and silver spiral hatpin becomes an item to be cherished as much for its appearance as for keeping a hat from blowing away in the wind.

UNDER THE DOGWOOD TREE

In a small house painted in soft hues of pink and bluish gray, a woman surrounds herself with things as whimsical in nature as the cards she designs. Articles of enchantment are found throughout her property. In her garden of creeping phlox, purple salvia, foxgloves, morning glories, and herbs, a shady path leads past three cast-iron duck sentries to the pale blue door of a miniature pink cottage. Complete with a small spiderweb window and decorated with tiny running rabbits, visitors are always enticed by the shed's magic and are surprised to find mere garden tools within. Another charming little cottage is found under her dogwood tree. There, a colorful fantasy birdhouse with exaggerated tilts and angles, built by the artist, is occasionally inhabited by feathered friends. "Children love coming here," she says, "and I guess that's because I keep the child in me very much alive."

The artist began drawing at the age of three, encouraged by her mother's passion for watercolors, and inspired by her grandmother's garden and her father's storytelling. Combining this heritage with images from her travels, she is well supplied with ideas when she sits down to create something new.

"My grandmother was a great collector. She lived in a three-story farmhouse chock full of wonderful things, and was a painter as well. I am the third generation of women in my family to develop my painting and design talents. With such role models, I hardly see how things could have turned out otherwise, nor would I have wanted them to."

A favorite place to sketch is on a little deck astride her kitchen. Early in the mornings, one can find the table overlooking her garden laid out with colored pencils and sketchpads. It is here that the artist sits, completing works inspired from her travels throughout the country and abroad. "I like to stand right on the spot and draw because I have to capture the soul of a place by being there. Then I take my sketches home and finish them."

Although her studio at home also faces her flower and herb garden, she finds the table under the dogwood tree irresistible when its blossoms begin to fall. "It's almost musical out there then, all those dogwood petals in motion and the wonderful dancing light. It reminds me of a line from one of my favorite poets, Gerard Manley Hopkins: 'Glory be to God for dappled things.'"

Under the leafy canopy of a dogwood tree, left, a table is laid out for joyful hours of sketching. This little deck overlooking a flower and herb garden is an artist's favorite spot to create works as enchanting and colorful as the little tilted bird cottage sitting on the rail.

The potting room, left, is a version of the traditional conservatory where plants were tended to all year. A southern exposure provides steamy warmth even in deepest winter. Pots, potting soil, nutrients, and bulbs for forcing are handily stored under the wide coun- tertop. Baskets and other containers for flowers are also in abundance. ❧ The challenge of the miniature rose, above, is that it will tempera- mentally turn yellow and drop its leaves if not watered to its liking. But in the care of the knowledgeable gardener, it delights.

The farmhouse kitchen probably stood where it did as a matter of accident or haphazard choice; yet its situation might have been planned by a master-strategist in farmhouse architecture. Dairy and poultry-yard, and herb garden, and all the busy places of the farm seemed to lead by easy access into its wide flagged haven, where there was room for everything and where muddy boots left traces that were easily swept away. And yet, for all that it stood so well in the centre of human bustle, its long, latticed window, with the wide window-seat. . . looked out on a wild spreading view of hill and heather and wooded combe. The window nook made almost a little room in itself, quite the pleasantest room in the farm as far as situation and capabilities went.

Saki
The Cobweb

Artists make no distinction about where they pour their creativity, and do so with the same intensity and passion for detail that they apply to their regular disciplines. Marjorie Kinnan Rawlings, author of *The Yearling*, cooked up splendid feasts in the kitchen of her humble Florida farmhouse, Cross Creek, left, now a museum. At Cross Creek, the author never failed to admire the ever changing view outside her kitchen window. Whether orchestrating feasts with vegetables from her garden, or writing on the back porch, she regarded the creative process as being one with the beauty of nature. "Writing is my profession, my exaltation and my torture. I write as an introvert, attempting to turn an intangible loveliness into a tangible conception," she explained. "But I cook as an extrovert, singing at the top of my lungs, in ecstasy and the certainty of fulfillment." Inspired by her place of residence, the author also published an account of her life on the farm, *Cross Creek*, and a book of recipes entitled *Cross Creek Cookery*. 🐝 Ingredients and utensils for baking, above, await the cook. The well-worn mixing bowl has turned out many magnificent cakes, kept fresh in a cake server with a leafy surface as glossy as boiled frosting.

A PLACE FOR FAVORITE THINGS

a flea market curio evokes delight beyond understanding. Four cherubic faces in silver frames become a tableau of childhood captured on a table. A great-grandmother's tureen, used at every family celebration, becomes rich with meaning as time goes by. Favorite things are those that never fail to strike what Abraham Lincoln called "the mystic cords of memory."

Living in the midst of meaningful objects links us to the past and its heightened sensibility. These precious mementos have provenance, which curators determine by documenting the ancestry of strangers. But within these pages, provenance is a matter of personal history, of objects that come down to us as family heirlooms or are collected during a lifetime of wandering in and out of tempting little shops and coming upon unexpected yard sales.

What are our favorite things? Lace of course—webs of crochet spun in thin air, infinitesimally fine rosepoint, crisp petals of Irish Carrickmacross—with a sensuous texture to appreciate with the fingertips. Flowers are another, dried or fresh, for they never fail to lift the spirit. Others are objects of beauty, like vintage summer whites and wide-brimmed straws drooping with silken roses.

And then there are collections, joyful little assemblages on a table, bookshelf, or mantelpiece that tell a fascinating story without words. Some gatherings are family reunions, like a closet full of blue-and-white china in all its glorious varieties. Other collections seem to have no relation at all, but mingle compatibly nonetheless, the whimsical alongside the precious, pulled together by the mystic cords of memory. Victorian bibliophile Augustine Birrell used to give this advice to bookbuyers but it applies to all pursuit of favorite things: "Good as it is to inherit . . . it is better to collect . . ."

G iving joy even when not in use, this collection of hats is displayed, left, on a wrought-iron tree at the entrance to the bath suite in designer Jessica McClintock's home. Her signature is romance, translated here in voluptuous folds of silken roses and French ribbon.

When it rained or snowed, Charles would direct his horse over the shortcuts. . . . every night he would come home to a glowing fire, the table set, the furniture arranged comfortably, and a charming woman, neatly dressed, smelling so fresh you wondered where the fragrance came from and whether it wasn't her skin lending the scent to her petticoat.

She charmed him by a number of elegant gestures. Sometimes it was a new way of cutting paper sconces for the candles, a flounce that she changed on her dress, or the extraordinary name of some quite simple dish that the maid had spoiled but that Charles swallowed with pleasure down to the bitter end. In Rouen she saw some women wearing charms on their watches; she bought charms. She wanted two large vases of blue glass on her fireplace, and awhile later, an ivory workbox with a vermeil thimble. The less Charles understood those elegant touches, the more he responded to their attraction. They added something to his sensual pleasures and to the sweetness of his home. It was as if gold dust were being spread all along the narrow path of his life.

Gustave Flaubert
Madame Bovary

Late nineteenth-century cotton eyelet nightgowns and shawls take a morning sunbath on a stairway landing. The eyelet slip on the hanger was found in an antiques shop in Brighton, England. The chair, discovered in a secondhand store, was painted with a matte finish ivory, then upholstered in muslin. Its crowning touch is a piece of trapunto embroidery on linen with an unusually high satin stitch relief, brought home from Sweden by the owner.

The manner in which collections are displayed always adds to their appeal. In the corner created by interior designer and shop owner Charlotte Moss, left, a salute to roses is gallantly made in a fragrant passageway. A jewellike moiré ribbon in deepest rose festoons the elegant trio of gilt-framed botanical prints like a crown. The prints themselves form a beribboned picture tree, a theme underscored by the trio of miniature standard trees. A romantic bowl painted with well-furled cabbage roses is filled with rose petal potpourri, sending a fragrant message that within lives one who adores roses. ❧ As Alice in Wonderland would say, "curiouser and curiouser." Her comment could be the theme of a collection, above, where nothing is quite what it seems, yet is altogether totally delightful. Wooden eggs nest on a piece of mercury glass, incubating under a bell jar. A tiny petitpoint pillow designed and created by the collector is inspired in turn by a favorite piece of finespun filet lace. The imposing rounds are antique drapery tiebacks. "I'm a soft touch for the bright and shiny," confesses the homeowner. The early American marbles, hand rolled out of clay and then fired, are never perfectly round. They possess what author Willa Cather expressed as "that irregular and intimate quality of things made entirely by the human hand."

Some people collect silver and gold; others collect humble things that call to them on walks through the outdoors, a yen that keeps their eyes on the roam. Collections formed from nature are unique in that they rarely have a price tag, and the humblest of objects is made beautiful by the artistry of the human hand. Near the mantel-by-the-sea, above, heaped with shells from beachcombing around the world, one can almost hear the ocean roar. Pink geraniums grow amusingly out of an antique fisherman's creel, shells adorn a wreath, and a hilarious toby jug with a trout for a handle is perched among the seaweed. A molded sand castle with flags flying is an endearing version of the one every lover of the sea has built, a permanent rendition of all those temporary wonders. When a special passion is displayed with such creativity and humor, the results can be spectacular. 🐦 Under a tall and slender myrtle topiary, right, a congress of birdhouses perches on a hallway table. The collector is a photographer's stylist and whenever she is in the country on a shoot, she looks for birdhouses at yard sales or roadside stands. She finds birds' nests on the ground that have fallen from trees, or sometimes perfect ones still intact in the winter, when the leaves as well as the birds are gone. "The nests," she explains, "were deserted. I do not leave any birds homeless."

A LOVE FOR LACE

A husband and wife, both of them artisans and designers, have a special passion for crocheted doilies, runners, and tablecloths, for like so many of their generation, they have childhood memories of watching these items being created by women in their families. The collection of laces they own represents two centuries of home crochet. The oldest and most prized of their collection is a piece created by the husband's great-grandmother as she awaited the birth of her first child. With fine gauge of thread and crochet hook, the tablecloth took an entire winter to complete.

When this country was settled, women from all parts of Europe brought their lace-making traditions with them. In many a lonely farmhouse, yearning for a bit of beauty, women crocheted something delicate to cover a bare table or windowpane, to take the edge off the roughness of a new existence. The tradition became institutionalized, and every ladies' magazine included patterns for making lacy objects of adornment. A tablecloth crocheted from a magazine pattern of the popular pinwheel was found by the collectors at a junk store in the late 1960s, when these ubiquitous homemade laces were out of fashion. Now these pieces are rarely found for sale, and command high prices. The most recent addition to their collection is an ecru-colored tablecloth made by a woman in the couple's New England town. The wife explains: "I bought the tablecloth from her not just because it was beautiful, but because I loved the fact that she was making a living in her home in that way."

The tablecloths are used frequently, even for picnics, and are not difficult to launder. They are washed by hand with old-fashioned soap powder and a dry bleach, and given a rinse in gentle sizing instead of starch. While still damp, they are stretched on a stretcher with an adjustable wooden frame studded with tiny nails, on which the edges of the lace are gently hooked. The pieces then dry to a brilliant white in the sun.

Mending worn lace is also part of the joy of collecting, and a frequent one, for century-old crochet often needs some gentle repair, particularly between the circles. The great-grandmother's tablecloth has a couple of circles that are missing. "But," her descendant says, "we have crochet hook and thread ready to go. Sooner or later, everything gets done."

Crocheted tablecloths, left, evoke the image of a woman at home spinning lace around her finger with little more than a hook and thin air. The damask linen napkins were a wedding gift, and are used not just for company but on a regular basis for family dinners.

*T*o collect anything, no matter what, is the healthy human impulse
of man and boy, and the longer and harder the search,
the greater the joy of acquisition.

Agnes Repplier
Times and Tendencies

Some collections fit no genre at all, adhering only to a certain well-defined aesthetic. On a bedside table, left, a finely woven towel is offset by the simple floral arrangements. The botanical print, with a touch of the owner's favorite blue, was picked up in England. Precious photographs are kept in a leafy white dish.

🐦 The mantel, above, is like a family diary. As a child, the wife used to wear white gloves to Sunday school: "I loved the tradition, how clean and fresh they looked, and when my husband saw this white hand-held vase, he bought it for me as an anniversary present." Both husband and wife are potters, and the handpainted terracotta candlestick is a product of their studio. The chintz lampshade, trimmed with a silk fringe, was made by the husband in high school. Although at first sight the three objects are unrelated, the history they weave makes them a meaningful tableau.

The cupboard, left, fairly vibrates with its brightly colored contents of majolica pottery, a cornucopia of lettuce- and gingko-leaf plates, purple-tinged scallop shells, cherries, peaches, and a spectacular sunflower cake plate. The collector loves majolica for its fanciful, naturalistic motifs and strong colors, as well as for the energy it generates. Since she found her first majolica—still her favorite piece—eighteen years ago in a Florida town, she has become an expert in collecting this once-popular Victorian pottery. "Majolica was everywhere," she says, "because it was given in the late nineteenth-century as bonuses with soap and baking powder. Many American pieces were made by obscure potters who never marked their own work, but you learn to recognize them." ❧ Precious English flow blue china, with its colors that melt into each other, was a new form of firing originally produced by mistake. The china mingles with delightfully mismatched English teacups, above. The collector's passion is for "English Primrose," a made-up term for English china of the 1920s and '30s featuring tiny handpainted spring flowers. The blue flowered cup to the far left is "very old, a great-grandmother teacup." The cup with the orange flowers is the sole and saucerless survivor of her mother's everyday china. The miniature clown saltshaker is French, and the eggcup with cats was discovered in an antiques shop in Greenwich Village.

WHITE VESSELS
FOR A SOFT LOOK

An affinity for the spectrum of white, from its purest state to taupe, is seen throughout a tranquil home by the shore. The colors are oyster, cream, and palest lemon yellow, which give the rooms a glow even on a cloudy day. In this venerable house, where original features are lovingly allowed to show their age, every detail contributes to its owner's love of grace and lightness of being. Century-old wainscotting and molding are given a dignified white stripe, and the wood floors are bleached and silvery. Throughout the house, rooms are minimally furnished, although there is never a feeling of emptiness.

"I don't like objects that are just for display, and I don't leave them about. I'm tidy that way. I have two little boys, but even before they came into my life, I kept my surfaces spare. It's my Swedish sensibility. The house is very light, and because I like beautiful things, I keep my rooms feeling simple and fresh so I am also able to collect things."

And what does this owner collect? As a publicist, she travels a great deal, and she looks for another piece of all-white glazed pottery to add to her collection wherever she goes. She likes the shapes of vessels such as vases, pitchers, bowls, or gravy boats, although a flat serving piece sometimes proves irresistible. Regardless of the shape, she is drawn to white pieces that perform a service. Over the years her assemblage has grown to overflowing, spanning oceans and centuries as she sought out pieces of French creamware, English ironstone, American stoneware, and virtually any form of white glazed pottery.

Her gleaming white treasures are stored in nearby cabinets, handy to the needs of flower gatherers home from a walk. Country-house vases are in high demand, from the appearance of the first wild roses of May to the last of October's asters and gentian. And in the height of summer when the corn and tomatoes are ripe, extra leaves expand the table and every bowl, pitcher, and tureen is put into service. All the disparate white pieces nicely harmonize, adding a bit of elegance to the sandy-footed casualness of a summer feast.

Angelique tulips, left, are displayed in an English porcelain pitcher atop a plate rack from the 1800s. The white treasures, above, are a glazed pitcher from the '20s, a small porcelain cup, an Irish china fruit bowl, and a traditional English milk pitcher.

Keeping treasured albums current, left, is an ongoing task, and one that a family enjoys when the weather keeps them indoors. When the children are visited by their grandmother, they enjoy cozying up on the couch and having her point out photographs of their parents when they were young. Calligraphy's measured beauty speaks of an age when time moved more slowly, and of a world where there was ample time for the graceful curve. The flowing lines, above, turn thoughts into endearing keepsakes to be admired.

Learning the language of flowers became the life-long passion of a woman who loves to adorn her home with them, in both their fresh and everlasting states. The blooming herbs, peonies, and roses, above, were picked while still wet with morning dew. ❧ Her wreath at the window, right, is made of an assortment of herbs. Dried cockscomb, lavender, and hydrangeas, as well as her old-fashioned favorites of zinnia, delphinium, and peonies are presented in vase and baskets.

❧ The shade of an unusual wicker lamp, opposite, shelters a cherished collection. The baby photos sweetly mingle with baby cups, favorite china toys, and other keepsakes from childhood. A photo of the ancestral homestead in the corner is given a resplendent silver wreath, and reigns over the scene.

*T*here were India shawls suspended, curtain-wise, in the parlour door, and curious fabrics, corresponding to Gertrude's metaphysical vision of an opera-cloak, tumbled about in the sitting-places. There were pink silk blinds in the windows, by which the room was strangely be-dimmed; and along the chimneypiece was dis-posed a remarkable band of velvet, covered with coarse, dirty-looking lace. "I have been making myself a little comfortable," said the Baroness, much to the confusion of Charlotte, who had been on the point of proposing to come and help her put her superfluous draperies away. But what Charlotte mistook for an almost culpably delayed subsidence Gertrude very presently per-ceived to be the most ingenious, the most interest-

ing, the most romantic intention. "What is life, indeed, without curtains?" she secretly asked herself.

Henry James
The Europeans

*A*uthentic Victorian lace curtains are a rar-ity, because of exposure to elements and the way they were hung, pulled back and liter-ally screwed into the wall. More likely to be found are Irish Carrickmacross, double and tri-ple stitched at every raised rosette. A length of crisp Irish Carrickmacross is used, above, as an ivy-bedecked halo to a prized framed piece of nineteenth-century cutwork lace at holiday time. 🌿 An inviting veil of lace at the win-dow is the essence of the feminine aesthetic, softening and gentling the architectural lines. The tendency of women to prefer the curved and sinuous to the straight and right-angled is described by the poet John Greenleaf Whittier as the single greatest difference between men and women. "Our hard, stiff lines with her," he said, "are flowing curves of beauty." The ele-gant roman shade with its lovely rosepoint bor-der, right, is a celebration of grace, and the delicacy of the curtain is echoed in the clustered petals of the Queen Anne's lace.

A PLACE FOR DREAMS

*i*n a place for dreams, the childhood prayer "Now I lay me down to sleep" is breathed with a sigh that relinquishes all cares. Beds are dressed in fine linen and lace of a white so dazzling that even in the dark of night the room has the glow of moonlight. Awakening is a gentle affair when gossamer sheers at the window subdue the brightness of the morning sun.

In the youthful Land of Counterpane, the bed and its coverlet become an entire world. A night's sleep in such a room turns one into the "child of the pure, unclouded brow and dreaming eyes of wonder" described by Lewis Carroll. In the rooms within these pages, that transformation is assured. Whether spare or sumptuous, they are places of peace like a cradle gently rocking, where bed linen, soft and scented, touches the slumberer with a whisper of tenderness, evoking lines from a poem by Rupert Brooke: "The cool kindliness of sheets, that soon, smooth away trouble."

Counterpanes are inspired by dreams from the past: a Marseilles spread from Tivoli, heavy with stitchery; a featherweight duvet, delicately embroidered; patchwork, appliqué, and crochet all evoke things from a gentler world.

Of all the intimate spaces, the bedroom is the most private and the most soothing. Its purpose is rest, and its sole message comfort. The vision of its surroundings is the first image that meets the eye in the morning and the last image to follow one into the land of dreams, a vision so soothing it beckons one to sink deep into past memory and once again experience the deep slumber and complete peace of a sleeping child.

In a place for dreaming, some rooms are simple and spare. Others are elegantly Gothic, with majestic mahogany posts holding a nest of bedcovers heaped high with ruffles and feathers. Whatever the style, the room for a sweet night's repose should exude a feeling of both peaceful completion and joyful renewal.

A sleeping nook high up under the eaves, left, recalls a lullaby and memories of a cradle in the treetop, curtained by whispering leaves. Blue-and-white curtains that swag gracefully from a peg rack heighten the privacy of this retreat at the top of the house.

Dorothea walked about the house with de-lightful emotion. . . .

"Now, my dear Dorothea, I wish you to favour me by pointing out which room you would like to have as your boudoir," said Mr. Casaubon . . . [and] led the way thither. . . .

The chairs and tables were thin-legged and easy to upset. It was a room where one might fancy the ghost of a tight-laced lady revisiting the scene of her embroidery. A light book-case contained duodecimo volumes of polite literature in calf, completing the furniture.

"Yes," said Mr. Brooke, "this would be a pretty room with some new hangings, sofas, and that sort of thing. A little bare now."

"No, uncle," said Dorothea, eagerly. "Pray do not speak of altering anything. There are so many other things in the world that want altering—I like to take these things as they are. And you like them as they are, don't you?" she added, looking at Mr. Casaubon. "Perhaps this was your mother's room when she was young."

"It was," he said, with his slow bend of the head.

George Eliot
Middlemarch

In a tranquil summer-home bedroom, soft green walls offset creamy bed linen and glazed pottery like a leaf to a lily. The ocean light illuminates paisley tree-of-life panels executed in finely spun nets of filet crochet. The all-white bedspread is richly embroidered in Marseilles style, and the glazed pottery pieces are flea market finds.

One of the most delightful features of the Edwardian style is its use of pillows, pillows, and more pillows. A nest of gossamer pillows is piled doubly high on a counterpane feathery with lace, left. The embroidered sheers at the window softly filter the morning light for those who gently slumber between the graceful mahogany posts. 🌿 Extra pillows tied with ribbons, above, are stacked on a chair and on an oaken bucket, awaiting the unexpected guest.

L inen is the fiber of sleep, and its ability to retain light is its great charm. In this all-white room, left, the glory of linen and lace makes its own serene statement. White walls adorned with two simple prints form a quiet backdrop for the otherwise sumptuously attired room. Cutwork-edged voile panels imported from France dress the windows. An enchanting featherbed counterpane with a wide border and panels of flowing cutwork lace drapes a bed made up with soft damask sheets, ruffled shams of fine batiste and filet crochet embroidered borders, and a gentle mound of folded duvet.

Lavishness and luxury are also the features of the breakfast table, above, where white roses and tulips make an airy bouquet in three crystal champagne glasses.

A GUEST'S WARM WELCOME

Part of the joy of welcoming a beloved friend or relative into one's home is in the preparation. Providing amenities a traveler often doesn't think to pack or has no room for in a suitcase demonstrates thoughtfulness on the part of the host. Bathrooms are graced with toiletries, an abundance of towels, and, on the back of the door, a thick and cozy terrycloth bathrobe. In the bedroom, plenty of empty dresser drawers and hangers are essential. The bed is dressed with the best linens and the bed table is provided with a good reading lamp. An easy chair is placed in a quiet corner to allow curling up with a book undisturbed. On a desk, there are writing materials and postage stamps. Also, there can be a photo album to evoke fond memories of a shared past, and cards from mutual friends to warm the heart. A basket of fresh fruit, another holding flowers—nothing has been forgotten to provide a guest with all the comforts of home.

When people travel, they need a private sanctuary where they can collect their thoughts and restore themselves after the rigors of a long journey. A tranquil and calming room allows the traveler to acclimate to a new environment and savor the love and graciousness of another home. To be able to retreat to a pleasant place to rest, reflect, read, or have an intimate conversation with a friend or family member enhances any social visit. No matter how close one may be to one's host, prolonged stays can take their toll. When a place of one's own made personal by the presence of meaningful mementos is offered, a guest can choose to be solitary when the need arises. Special touches and preparation for comfort and privacy say "welcome to our home, stay awhile, and hurry back, for we love having you here."

What could be more welcoming after a long journey than a refreshing pick-me-up, above, of shortbread cookies, fresh strawberries, and light strawberry wine? ❧ The thoughtful space, right, top, includes a stack of inviting books, a nest of lacy pillows, and even a bottle of lavender water. The hand-stitched quilts on the bed and table provide a cozy feeling. ❧ A guestroom furnished with more than a bed, right, bottom, is the best way to make a person feel at home. The dresser has a hinged top that can become a writing desk. All the details here are chosen to please the eye as well as provide comfort, from the delicate needlepoint rug on the floor to the scalloped border of roses on the ceiling.

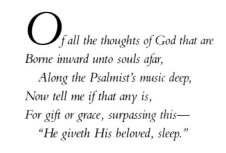

*O*f all the thoughts of God that are
Borne inward unto souls afar,
　　Along the Psalmist's music deep,
Now tell me if that any is,
For gift or grace, surpassing this—
　　"He giveth His beloved, sleep."

Elizabeth Barrett Browning
The Sleep

In an all-white bridal bedroom, the bed is swathed in a gauzelike wedding veil. The multiple borders of the lace mantelcloth and Gothic cradle are blessings for a fruitful marriage. Although the room is now part of a museum, one of Mobile, Alabama's finest surviving antebellum cottages, the characters of the original inhabitants are indelibly impressed upon the present scene.

The simple bedroom, left, is flooded with light from its four windows. The owner believes that a bedroom should serve solely as a place for rest and has eliminated all but the essentials. Except for the pale pink bed linens and the bright Canterbury bells on a chair, whites dominate the room. The light colors, the clean lines of the furniture, and the gleaming bare floors add to the pristine quality of the room. 🐾 Tapestry pillows, above, elegantly grace a high Edwardian bedroom with their deep, rich, Tudor colors. Even on the coldest winter night, the glowing fabrics will warm a counterpane. When these dark fabrics were used in homes before the turn of the century, they were often lost in the general darkness of the Victorian interiors. Matched with white linens, the fabrics are stunning. 🐾 When

rooms are kept spare and simple, the details of intricate and unusually beautiful needlework, above, are enhanced. The quilt with its unique color scheme of pale ecru, cream, and coral is heavy with infinitisimal stitches. The lavishly embroidered pillowcases and cutwork doily reveal the hand of a true artist. These pieces are treasured heirlooms, the work of a gifted aunt.

WAKING UP TO BEAUTY

A young woman carries on a family tradition by filling her Victorian home with lacy finery. With a grandmother who edged practically everything with tatted and crocheted lace, and a mother who is an antiques dealer specializing in vintage frocks and lace, she is the third generation carrying on a lovely legacy. Inheriting their passion for linens and lace as well as their collections, she graces almost every room of her residence with beautiful pieces.

"None of my linens are just for show—I use them all," she states. Many of the tablecloths from her linen collection hang from dowels to adorn her dining room walls. In her two-year-old daughter's nursery, lacy towels serve as valances and tablecloths as curtains. The crib and heirloom bassinet are embellished with Swiss eyelet stitched in place by the little girl's grandmother.

The owner's own bedroom is an enchanting sanctuary of lacy canopy and counterpane bathed in lemon-colored light. The canopy, a gift from her mother, is one of the very finest pieces she has seen. It is actually a 138-inch oval tablecloth of linen, probably made in Brussels early in this century. "It was so beautiful I felt it had to be something to wake up to every day." The tablecloth's filet lace inserts depict frolicking nudes, causing the owner to remark: "I can only imagine what kind of conversation it once inspired around the dinner table!"

Most of this woman's bed linens are tablecloths dating from the 1870s to 1910. The side curtain is a English manorhouse piece from the turn of the century. The bedspread, found in Nantucket, is a resplendent example of Irish crochet. "The Irish crochet as Americans knit," says the owner. "They crochet with two needles rather than one hook, in a much more intricate form. One of the ways you can distinguish it immediately is by its raised rosette, usually in the form of layers of petals, similar to the raised knob on a fisherman's knit sweater but much, much finer."

This woman's inherited love for linens and lace keeps her searching for treasures, and like her mother and grandmother before her, the collector does not hesitate to give old objects a new use. "I find something that should be on a table or a bed and I might put it on the wall because it looks more beautiful that way. When you find certain things, you just have to buy them," she states. "Sometimes I think everything I've bought was with me in a past life, because it feels like it's home as soon as I bring it through the door."

An Irish crochet tablecloth, left, makes a splendid bedspread with its majestic border of hollow, raised rosettes. "I love the idea of finding new uses for old things," says the owner. A favorite piece is a linen tablecloth with lace inserts that serves as a canopy.

A room in Martha's Vineyard, above, with its whitewashed clapboard walls, seems more like a back porch than a bedroom. In fact, the house was once part of a summer camp that the owners converted, painting its murky interior and expanding a tiny upstairs loft into an inviting bedroom. Its wonderful feature is the spectacular view of a pond filled with swans and other wildlife, and beyond it, the Atlantic Ocean. "Visitors think of this as an enchanted place because of the vista, and so do we," says the wife. 🐝 Over the years, the couple has furnished the room with treasures found at island junk stores, antiques shops, and yard sales. Many of their favorites come from venerable old summer houses nearby. Above the bed one finds a row of these scavenged prizes, such as a tiny green candleholder that is a piece of nineteenth-century art glass, formerly part of a pair, but now cherished in its solitary state. Next to it, a fabulous lion looms over a snake—an irresistible find as both owners like things with a sense of contrast and humor. Completing the row of Vineyard treasures is a beautiful Art Deco plate picked up for $3 many years ago. The Majolica creamware lamp from the twenties, next to the bed, required many hours of repair, including the deft restoration of a missing cupid's arm, with polyester resin. A chair is painted a color called High Summer Blue (from a can of paint bought in England) which epitomizes the whole feeling of summer near the water. It was recently entered in the yearly Vineyard agricultural fair and won a prize. "I like to use old things until they wear out," says the wife. "I'm not interested in preserving them forever, and so very often they're not in perfect condition. But that's not really what's important. It's important to enjoy them and feel somehow connected to the past."

*E*very detail of decoration seemed to have
been thought out with loving care. Never had
wealth of adornment been more daintily disguised
in order to be translated into elegance, to be ex-
pressive of taste and incite to voluptuousness.
Everything there would have warmed the blood
of the chilliest mortal. The iridescence of the
hangings, whose colour changed as the eye
looked at them from different angles, now white,
now wholly pink, harmonized with the effects of
light infused into the diaphanous folds of the
muslin and produced an impression of mistiness.
The human soul is strangely attracted to white,
love has a delectation for red, and gold gives en-
couragement to the passions because it has the
power to realize their dreams. Thus all that is

vague and mysterious in man, all his unex-
plained affinities, found their involuntary sympa-
thies gratified in this boudoir. There was in this
perfect harmony a concerto of colour to which the
soul responded with ideas which were at once voluptuous, imprecise and fluctuating.

Honoré de Balzac
History of the Thirteen

The voluptuousness of lace is displayed,
left, with every comely detail high-
lighted by an underlayer of pale ecru silk. The
crisply tailored sheets underneath invite one into
a nocturnal world of fantasy. The exquisite
handiwork on the pillowcases and bedspread, as
well as the details on the bedside table, create an
abode of opulence. Even the lampshade is be-
decked with a bit of lace, and its light reflects off
the wall to cast a gentle golden glow upon the
room. The stenciled decorations on the wall do
not distract, but give a bit of fancy to the elegance. A white bouquet, a few leather-bound
classics, and a crystal decanter of wine complete
this perfect habitat for reading, sleeping, and
dreaming. ❧ Extra pillows adorn a mahogany armoire, above, which contrasts darkly
with the dazzling white of the pillows. The lines
of this dark, grained cabinet embody the grace
and fluidity of times past, with an emphasis on
simplicity and taste. The lacy pillows peeking
out give a feminine touch to an otherwise quite
masculine piece of furniture, with its angled
edges and formal demeanor.

A PLACE FOR BEAUTY

*d*evotion to beauty is a careful and daily tending, a ritual of polish and gentle refinement that takes place from bathing to dressing. In a place for beauty, a woman looks leisurely to her appearance and increases her allure. Such a pleasurable time deserves surroundings filled with grace.

Beauty is not only what she does, but what she touches. Therefore, a place for beauty is one of gracefully curved looking glasses and of tenderly painted cachepots sitting on a vanity, filled with cosmetic brushes. It is a place of glowing tortoiseshell and softly burnished silver brushes and combs, where washbasins are painted with roses delicate as bone china, and closets have no doors lest the beauty of their contents be concealed. Above all, a place for beauty is one where the sun is welcome by day, filtering through lacy curtains in the morning, and where before retiring at night, candles glimmer.

Victorians treated the daily ritual of bathing and dressing the same way they approached all aspects of everyday living, with a lavish appreciation for utilitarian beauty and an equally lavish love of the sensory. After the day began with a languid steep or under the invigorating needles of a shower, came the toilette, the measured application of cosmetics, jewelry, and perfume, an enhancement of the body before dressing.

Toilette, the devotion to beauty, is not practiced in a hurried way. A woman is seated in comfort before a vanity on which is laid everything needed to pamper, nurture, replenish, and protect her beauty. Prepared with creams and foundations, the face in the looking glass is the canvas on which a woman works her art. Palettes of color appear from a vanity drawer for a delicate brush of petal pink or soft lilac. Then, the skin is given a final polish with an airborne sprinkling of silken powder from a feathery pouf, a finish that will cause the face to glow with the inner beauty of porcelain. Finally, perfume, the heart note of a woman's soul, decanted in heavy cut-glass flacons, is applied. When a gentlewoman steps from her dressing room, the sweet results of her labor are for the world to behold.

I n a home by the seashore, the shell pink walls of the hallway to the gleaming bath and dressing room, left, give a feeling of entering into a chambered nautilus. The delicate towel rack and pristine blue-and-white rug are in keeping with the feeling of cleanliness.

I rose; I dressed myself with care: obliged to
be plain—for I had no article of attire that was
not made with extreme simplicity—I was still
by nature solicitous to be neat. It was not my
habit to be disregardful of appearance, or careless
of the impression I made; on the contrary, I ever
wished to look as well as I could, and to please
as much as my want of beauty would permit. I
sometimes regretted that I was not handsomer: I
sometimes wished to have rosy cheeks, a straight
nose, and small cherry mouth: I desired to be
tall, stately, and finely developed in figure; I felt
it a misfortune that I was so little, so pale, and
had features so irregular and so marked. . . .
However, when I had brushed my hair very
smooth, and put on my black frock—which,
Quaker-like as it was, at least had the merit of
fitting to a nicety—and adjusted my clean white
tucker, I thought I should do respectably enough
to appear before Mrs. Fairfax; and that my new
pupil would not at least recoil from me with
antipathy. Having opened my chamber window,
and seen that I had left all things straight and
neat on the toilet-table, I ventured forth.

Charlotte Brontë
Jane Eyre

S ome places for beauty take one fresh from
the bath to a makeup table. Here the feminine sentiment is portrayed in many gentle
curves: in the delicate marble-topped vanity
found in an antiques shop, the swoop of the
Roman shades strewn with tiny flowers, and the
commodious wicker chair.

This charming alcove with its pale blue and white stripes makes excellent use of a small and somewhat awkwardly angled space. Shaker-style pegs on the wall display dresses of lace and frills too ravishing not to be shown, eliminating the need for a closet. ❧ Objects of beauty such as the clear etched-crystal perfume bottles and the bone-handled brush and hand mirror are placed before the oval looking glass with its gracefully elongated shape. Seated before such resplendent objects evokes the poet Kahlil Gibran, who once wrote, "Beauty is eternity gazing at itself in a mirror."

A CLOSET WITHOUT DOORS

When clothing and linens are stored with beauty in a closet, there is no need for a door. A designer has created her space with a combination of artistry and practicality, incorporating attractive storage objects people often have but rarely use. Baskets, hat boxes, and trunks of all kinds are used to store ribbons, scarves, jewelry, belts, sewing things, remnants, "and all the little things you need to have handy but don't know what to do with," she says. A favorite type of container, inexpensive basket trays, are easy to find and retrieve. In a closet they can be stacked one on top of each other to hold small linens.

Her open, lace-adorned shelves are built next to a window, and sunny spaciousness aptly describes this spot in the mornings. The lace edging the owner uses on the top two shelves is of handmade crochet. The other shelves are lined with lace-edged tablecloths, providing extra protection for cashmere sweaters and precious clothing items. The designer finds small crochet-edged linen tea tablecloths to be a good size for shelves. Antique ribbons are plentiful in this closet as well. Around a bunch of lavender or a bundle of sheets, the ribbons offer a colorful touch to the wicker, creams, and whites that dominate the shelves.

The designer loves to have the antique accessories and parasols she collects on display. Two of her favorites are a late 1800s ivory silk-embroidered Chinese shawl with a fantastic fringe, and a cotton-lace parasol with a bamboo handle. These objects are often in plain view, draped over a chair by the window or standing against a wall of the closet.

The owner keeps her closet fragrant with open bowls and tea caddies filled with potpourri. The mixture of cedar chips, tansy, southernwood, rosemary, and other sweet-smelling herbs also serves to repel unwanted insects. Sprigs of lavender are tucked between the layers of neatly folded clothing and sheets. Lavender's strong but delicate fragrance permeates fibers and is the bane of moths. With so many precious things stored away so prettily, the liberal use of these fragrant herbs is both attractive and essential.

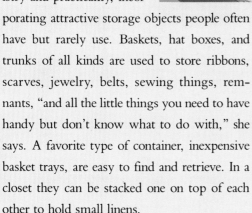

The closet without doors, left, has nothing to hide, with its lace-adorned shelves and pretty containers. 🌿 A dusty rose French ribbon with a sachet tucked into its bow, above, holds tea towels, and exemplifies the owner's love for beauty even in the smallest touches.

Entering into the corner bathing area, left, is like stepping into the past. The furnishings are the result of many years of collecting by a couple who loves to find old cast-offs and transform them into something sublime. Like vagabonds, they spent the early years of their marriage picking up at a bargain items like the fragile spindled dressing screen resplendent with old-fashioned bouquets. The enormous armoire is whimsically painted with the same scene as the view out the window, and serves as a clothes closet. And what better place to display a collection of antique mirrors? Cutwork-edged voile, above, lines the window adorned with a spray of orchids in an unstopped antique crystal bottle. Fresh white terry towels trimmed with roses and a spectacular spray of fringe cascade down whitewashed racks onto the old-fashioned footed tub.

A BATHROOM TRIMMED IN SENTIMENT

It was the bathroom that seduced a couple into buying a graceful old house outside of St. Louis. It is a big room on the second floor, and when husband and wife saw the light streaming in from the large window, they decided immediately that they wanted to live in this home. The owners wished to retain as well as enhance the lightness and cheerfulness of the room, so their color scheme included sunny peach for the walls and lots of white for the furnishings.

Collectors with a strong sense of history, the couple can't help but surround themselves with pieces that bring a memory or a smile, and fill their home with sentiment. The bathroom, decorated with precious objects, is one of the prettiest and most intimate rooms of their house. Every memento calls forth a story of its discovery, inheritance, or creation, to be shared with all who enter their friendly household.

Looking for treasures everywhere, the wife discovered an heirloom dress in an antiques store and made it an integral part of her own family's heritage, christening her two sons in it. The dress, an image that never fails to evoke fond memories, now hangs in the bathroom next to the cream-colored linens inherited from the wife's mother. A wicker table found in a small shop in Old St. Charles, near the Missouri River, is placed in front of the window, providing a wonderful display area for little items. The couple search continuously for collectibles that reflect their unique tastes. Husband and wife are both drawn to pieces with a tinge of romanticism and classicism, like a picture of two angelic cherubs, or tiny doll-sized frames protecting pressed butterflies. "The tiny butterflies in frames are another special memory," says the wife, "of the day we went to an auction where the contents of a wonderful old house in town were for sale—decades of accumulation including an enormous collection of butterflies."

With their finds from antiques shops, flea markets, and family attics, the couple also display works of their own. One particular piece is a slender wreath created by the wife. Made with dried grasses, blossoms, antique French ribbon, and a perfect rose, it hangs above the collection and enhances the personal atmosphere of the bathroom. Truly this is a room filled not just with sunlight, but with keepsakes that show the warm and loving hearts of the couple, and reflect their observation that "bathrooms are intimate in a different way."

A runner of Turkish carpet warming the old-fashioned octagonal bathroom tile of this venerable house, left, is truly Victorian-inspired. The window display area also enhances the intimacy of the room as each piece in the collection has a personal story to reveal.

Sometimes, when . . . Dolly his maid was making his bed, he came into his mother's room. It was as the abode of a fairy to him—a mystic chamber of splendour and delights. There in the wardrobe hung those wonderful robes—pink and blue and many-tinted. There was the jewel-case, silver-clasped, and the wondrous bronze hand on the dressing-table, glistening all over with a hundred rings. There was the cheval-glass, that miracle of art, in which he could just see his own wondering head and the reflection of Dolly (queerly distorted, and as if up in the ceiling), plumping and patting the pillows of the bed.

Oh, thou poor lonely little benighted boy! Mother is the name for God in the lips and hearts of little children.

William Makepeace Thackeray
Vanity Fair

In the lamplit dressing table, above, one finds objects in keeping with any elegant room: an Italian paper box of iridescent peacock blue and feathery tassel, flacons holding perfume, and a spill of antique jewelry. Under a window for good morning light, and well-lit by lamps in the evening, the all important finishing touches of the ritual of dressing are performed: a final light dusting of powder, the application of perfume from a resplendent cut-crystal flacon, and lastly, the choosing of a ring, a bracelet, or a beloved string of heirloom pearls. Then, with a last satisfied glimpse into the looking glass, beauty well tended, a gentlewoman steps from her dressing room into the world. ❧ The creator of the exquisite dressing corner, right, found three panels of rare nineteenth-century curtains at a sidewalk sale held by a woman "going minimal" on Manhattan's Upper West Side. "My bank was three blocks away," the owner says. "I had her hold everything and ran. I didn't know what I was going to do with the third panel, but I couldn't resist curtains so beautiful and hard to find." She swagged a window with two panels and draped the third, with a pale peach satin underlayer, over her thronelike dressing chair. Crystal and silver complement the exquisite lace. "I never had a minimal phase," says the owner, who has been collecting antique fabrics for years. "And the strange thing is, the more I layer and add, the more room there seems to be."

A PLACE OF HER OWN

a home can embody many places. It can be at once a retreat for solitude and personal pursuits, and a setting for favorite things, dreams, and beauty. The range of daily experience begs for an excursion to each of these places, and the challenge is to unify the diversity into a single home.

One homeowner has attempted this unification, cultivating her creative prowess to shape a place of her own. After two decades as a textile designer, she decided to forge a new career renovating houses. When she returned to her native city of Pittsburgh, she became enamored of a turn-of-the-century house whose exterior evoked the image of a Victorian Christmas card. The interior was dark and crowded with ultra-contemporary furniture, the honey pine floors were covered with carpets, but she understood its potential. However, as work on the renovation began, the owner realized that she could never sell the house.

"This house was meant for me," she explains. There seemed to be a place perfectly scaled for every one of her possessions and needs. In the sitting area, her artistic partiality for light is satisfied by French doors that provide ample illumination, forming a perfect environment for quiet hours in a ladder-back chair and a white sofa. A room in the third floor became a studio for her to pursue painting, enveloped by things that inspire her work. Here, an easel echoes the rich tones of the quilt curtains, and a canvas shows the influence of the prints and fabrics on the scrap screen and marble-topped iron table. In the bedroom, clusters of antique-framed photographs are as easily seen as the colorful quilts on the bed and tables. A secretary that doubles as a vanity sits by her bed. "It was amazing to me how all my things fit just right, like putting together a jigsaw puzzle, as if I had gone out and bought furniture for this house after measuring everything," she exclaims. The owner had purchased the house with the intention to resell, but as she poured energy and creativity into it, she transformed it into a place of her own. In this house, her many possessions were finally at home, as she was.

The art studio, left, is a retreat for creativity, decorated with things conducive to the artistic imagination. A scrap screen fills a corner and an iron table displays a collection of vintage fabrics. Quilts from a colorful collection curtain a wall of windows.

The white sofa bed, above, was essential to the home the owner raised her children in, but unnecessary in a new house with many bedrooms. Still, it fits with perfection into its new surroundings, and provides for many comfortable and sunny hours. The end table is a lap desk with stand, complete with leather writing surface, blotter, and inkwells. 🌺 In the sitting area, right, the artist embellishes her home with the fruits of her creative labors. The painting of a woman reclining on a beach was done in Nantucket. The ladder-back chair was a cast-off she rescued from the street. "It was covered with horrible metallic silver paint. Before I could finish stripping it, I had to gather up children, so there are still traces of paint on one of the bottom slats."

The handsome bedroom secretary, above left, was a reward for many months of exhausting renovation on the house. Its mirrors allow it to double as a vanity. 🐚 On the round table, above right, is a gathering of beloved family photographs. The potpourri bowl is a garage-sale treasure. Its porcelain flowers are painted in a childlike, naive quality that the artist loves. "I love the lack of sophistication and the simplicity of this bowl," she says. 🐚 The patchwork quilt, right, sums up the meaning of an intimate home. "I have been collecting quilts like this one since the sixties, when you could find them for a song," she explains. "I used to travel around and ask people where I could find them, and my search led me to a small town in Vermont where a woman sold me this beauty, done by her aunt. With the purchase came an aging piece of paper in which the aunt described the history of where and when the pieces of fabric she used in the quilt were found. When I put it on the bed in my newly renovated house, I realized that they both dated from the same time, the late 1800s. Although not everything here is of the same period, everything feels like it belongs to the house since time immemorial, not to be preserved but to be used and enjoyed. I cherish that little yellowing slip of paper."

PERMISSIONS AND PHOTOGRAPHY CREDITS

3: Photograph by Tina Mucci.

5: Photograph by Toshi Otsuki.

6: Photographs by William P. Steele (top, bottom), Luciana Pampalone (middle).

7: Photographs by William P. Steele (top, bottom), Michael Skott (middle).

8: Photograph by Toshi Otsuki.

10: Photograph by William P. Steele.

12–13: Excerpt from *Anne of Green Gables* by L.M. Montgomery. Copyright © 1908, 1935 by L.C. Page and Company. Reprinted by permission of Farrar, Straus and Giroux. Photograph by Michael Skott.

14: Photograph by Toshi Otsuki.

15: Photograph by Jim Hedrich.

17: Photograph by John Vaughan.

18–19: Photographs by William P. Steele.

20: Photograph by Jeff McNamara.

21: Photograph by William P. Steele.

22–23: Photographs by Joshua Greene.

24–25: Photograph by William P. Steele.

26: Photograph by William P. Steele.

27: Photograph by Michael Skott.

28: Photograph by William P. Steele. Excerpt from *To The Lighthouse* by Virginia Woolf. Copyright © 1927 by Harcourt Brace Jovanovich, Inc. and renewed 1955 by Leonard Woolf. Reprinted by permission of the publisher.

29: Photograph by Wendi Schneider.

30: Photograph by William P. Steele.

31: Excerpt from *A Room of One's Own* by Virginia Woolf. Copyright © 1929 by Harcourt Brace Jovanovich, Inc., and renewed 1957 by Leonard Woolf. Reprinted by permission of the publisher.

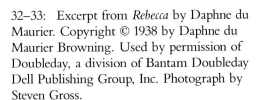
32–33: Excerpt from *Rebecca* by Daphne du Maurier. Copyright © 1938 by Daphne du Maurier Browning. Used by permission of Doubleday, a division of Bantam Doubleday Dell Publishing Group, Inc. Photograph by Steven Gross.

34: Photograph by Wendi Schneider.

35: Photograph by Tina Mucci.

36–37: Photographs by Pieter Estersohn.

38–39: Photograph by Luciana Pampalone.

40: Photograph by William P. Steele.

41: Photographs by Starr Ockenga (left), Jeremy Samuelson (right).

42: Photograph by Jim Hedrich.

44: Photograph by Toshi Otsuki.

45: Photograph by William P. Steele.

46: Photograph by Steven Gross and Sue Daley.

47: Photograph by Tom Pritchard. Excerpt from "The Cobweb" by Saki from *The Penguin Complete Saki*. Reprinted by permission of Viking Penguin Publishers.

48: Photograph by Jim Hedrich.

50–51: Photograph by Steven Gross.

52: Photograph by Jeff McNamara.

53: Photograph by Pieter Estersohn.

54: Photograph by Jim Hedrich.

55: Photograph by Steven Gross.

56: Photograph by William P. Steele.

58–59: Photographs by William P. Steele.

60: Photograph by Tina Mucci.

61: Photograph by Pieter Estersohn.

62–63: Photographs by Kari Haavisto.

64: Photograph by Kari Haavisto.

65: Photograph by Susie Cushner.

66: Photograph by Kari Haavisto (top), William P. Steele (bottom).

67: Photograph by John E. Kane.

68: Photograph by William P. Steele.

69: Photograph by Steven Gross.

70: Photograph by William P. Steele.

72–73: Photograph by Kari Haavisto.

74: Photograph by Jim Hedrich.

75: Photograph by William P. Steele.

76–77: Photographs by William P. Steele.

78–79: Photographs by William P. Steele.

80–81: Photograph by William P. Steele.

82: Photograph by Joshua Greene.

83: Photograph by William P. Steele (top), Toshi Otsuki (bottom).

84: Photograph by William P. Steele.

86–87: Photographs by Bryan E. McCay.

88–89: Photographs by William P. Steele.

90: Photograph by Kari Haavisto.

92–93: Photograph by Michael Skott.

94–95: Photographs by William P. Steele.

96: Photograph by Prashant Gupta.

97: Photograph by William P. Steele.

98–99: Photographs by William P. Steele.

100: Photograph by Jim Hedrich.

102: Photograph by Ralph Bogertman.

103: Photograph by Toshi Otsuki.

104: Photograph by William P. Steele.

106–107: Photographs by William P. Steele.

108–109: Photographs by William P. Steele.

110: Photograph by William P. Steele.

112: Photograph by Toshi Otsuki.